BRIAN FUGETT

Brian Fugett®

POEMS

CITIZENS FOR DECENT LITERATURE PRESS

Table of Contents

from the editors..ix
dedication xi

Easter Morning, 1989..1
Saturday Morning Cartoons 3
Interviewing Mr. Weck 5
At the Nursing Home 7
Rush Hour in Chula Vista..9
Buttercup in a Pick-up Truck 12
Sheltering Sheila 15
Peristalsis in the Bowels of Downtown 17
The Butcher On Third Avenue (2001) 19
Maroon Chevy..21
Titanium Hip Concerto in C Major 23
The Danger of Deaf Bartenders....................................25
Nicotine Wiggle of the Carcinogen Cowboy 27
Insomniac's Mantra...29
Vicious Wishes 30
Healthy Enough for Sex..31
Yesterday...32
First Kiss Awkwardness 33
Darwinian Nuns & The Embryo Orphanage 34
Dangerous Night..35
Art Lesson 101 36
Refrigerated Whispers Perpetuate the Revolution......37
Expiration Date..39
Dangling at her Mercy...40
If I was an Ice Cream Flavor I'd be:.............................41
Missing the Magic of My Youth....................................42
That Special Girl 43

A Winter Poem...44

We Are Art...45

Burning Desire to Evolve..................................46

Over the Years...47

Hangover 2017 48

Every Damn Night 49

My Favorite Barfly...50

Filling the Void...51

Crooked Smile 101..52

Ohio Boy Walkabout..53

Fast Food Friend..54

Affirmation of Self 55

Knock It Out of the Ballpark 56

Lincoln's Beard 57

Napalm Cochlea Enema 58

The Letter "P" Pisses Me Off 59

Barstool Philosopher..60

Nocturnal Cough Syrup Crusade 61

Throat Punch Butchers.....................................62

Oozing Crayola Red...63

Aggressive Swimmers..64

She Was Known As Flipper 65

Tracing the Scars 66

Bloodletting in the Hood..................................67

The Twitch in My Tail......................................68

The Social Badlands...69

A Flood of Circumstance..................................70

Picking at Scabs 71

Fornication Flashbacks......................................72

That One Date 73

Celluloid Serpent..74

Better Than French Cinema...............................75

Absorbing Her Aura 76
One of Those Nights..77
Braving the Storm..78
Time to Dump the Garbage..79
Perfectly Planned Catastrophe 80
Social Sisyphus Syndrome...81
Be My Special Predator 82
Bitchy Cat 83
The Cleansing 84
Vices 85
21st Century Gladiators 86
Inebriated Sacrifice 87
Bloody Mop Wringer..88
Forensic Plumber 89
Huff & Puff 90
My Vulcan Mojo...91
The Aftermath Equation 92
Betty Crocker Shank...93
Damaged Goods Dominatrix 94
Chronic Sinusitis: I am a nasal cripple 95
Coffee at the Two-Cup-Café 97
Deaf Tone Bouquet..99
Phantom Girlfriend 100
The Power of Words.. 101
That Girl Holding A Can of Spam 102
Confessions.. 103
Cluttered with Confusion 104
Special Night.. 105
Beware... 106
That One Gal.. 107
Sculpting an Identity... 108
Dive Bar Therapy... 109

A Bar Full of Poetry 110

The Ventriloquist 111

Apartment Life Curse 112

On the Brink of a Crisis 113

The Beds We Make 114

That Life Thingie 115

Running to the Grave 116

Art of the Sucker Punch 117

Brass Knuckles 118

Embezzling Kisses in the Rectory 119

A Different Lens 120

I Never Suffer 121

Slow Burn 122

Hand Grenades of Infatuation 123

Mapping the Anatomy of Lust 124

Diving Into Divorce 125

Time Clock Cancer 126

Mirrors 127

Chucking the Fallen Fruit 128

The Art of Suffering 129

Ambient Charm 130

Swallow Your Feelings 131

Perpetual Trick or Treat 132

Tug Job 133

Lethal Night 134

Finding Comfort 135

Fixed Bayonet 136

Razor Blade Theology 137

Truth Be Told 138

Two Spliff Whif 139

Real Gone Chick 140

Untitled 141

Absorbing the Glow 142
Recognize Your Shadow 143
The Pulse of Poetry 144
Running with the Jackals 145
Take a Peek 146
Silent Echo 147
Lip Gloss Lust 148
Ragged Morning 149
Kung Fu Cowboy 150
Duck Season 151
Deriving Sustenance 152
Things Remembered 153
Fortune Cookie Logic 154
Spent Matches 155
Terminal Floatation 156
Smothered By It 157
100 Dead Babies 158
The Ones You Notice 159
Absorbing the Locals 160
Mending the Discord 161
Two Seats Over 162
Brain Twitch 163
Riding the Buzz 164
The Way She Flows 165
No Way to Escape 166
Jukebox Blaring & Booze 167
Soccer Moms are Toxic 168
Making Subtle Power Moves 169
A Symphony of Ridicule 170
Under Her Breath 171
Ozone Layer Innuendo 173
Living on the Fringe 174

At the Bus Stop 175
Innocence Lost... 176
The Light Fades.. 177
Where the Fleas Sleep 178
Toxic Relationship.. 179
Chalk Lines Fade... 180
Starbucks Tourette's 181
Dead Page... 182
Here Comes the Flood.. 183
Icky Rules 184
Wrinkles & Scars 185
This is the Damn Poem 186

About the Author... 189

FROM THE EDITORS

When Michele and I first started talking about this book it felt right. Brian Fugett's sudden passing left me thinking about how selfless he was as a writer and publisher. He poured his heart into making books, into giving a voice to the fringe, and making everyone laugh in the process. He rarely shared his own work.

The bulk of this book was painstakingly transcribed from both of his social media pages. I won't lie, it was heartbreaking work. Here was my friend of 19 years, gone in an instant, and the poems hit differently. This book will give you a window into Brian's life—his depth, his philosophy, and his ability to describe what he sees with a strange clarity.

I want to thank Michele for trusting me to do this work and for often being the first person I talk to in the morning. Thank you to Andrew Lander for an amazing cover. When we knew we were doing this book, we both thought of him first because Brian loved his art. We hope you enjoy this time capsule of our friend and small press icon. Somewhere, he is wearing a shit-eating grin and cackling. Just the way it should be.

—Aleathia Drehmer

Books have a life cycle all their own—something that I learned over the years, and not without the influence of one fantastic and absolutely weird publisher by the name of Brian W. Fugett.

Many a time, I gave him shit for not having a collection of his own...but despite regular urging, it never came to be. Looking back at the poetry he amassed over the years, I see now why it wasn't time yet. The arc is there—if you respect it and wait for it.

It wasn't long after the sudden and early departure of our friend that I knew: it was time to birth this book baby. If not for him, as he looks on from beyond, then for those he left behind. In remembering, in celebration.

Special thanks to my bestie Aleathia, for her outstanding transcribing skills, but more importantly, the unwavering support and friendship. A special thanks also to Andrew Lander, who really did us a solid with a fitting portrait to cap off this tribute.

It is my sincere honor to present this collection. I believe the fucker would approve.

—Michele McDannold

In memory of my dad who was the first to encourage my curiosity, imagination, and creativity. Whenever I write I'm writing for you, I hope it makes you proud.

ॐ

Pops,

Thanks for inspiring my hobbies, interests, and future. I love sharing some of the same interests as you like history, sports, musical taste, and sense of humor/comedy. You were always there for me when I was down or wanted to have a conversation, whether serious or very unserious, or when I wanted to share a silly thought or song I liked. And I loved every time you shared those with me. I'll miss texting you random updates about my life, or about how bad our favorite sports teams are. I don't think I'll ever stop reaching for my phone to text you whenever I see a stupid headline, or I do something cool, or more likely stupid.

Love, Butler (Dylan).

Easter Morning, 1989

the taste of sleep
lingers in my mouth
as i feed another
cup of black coffee
to an impending ulcer.

uncle ernie with his
bushy gray hair
& crumb speckled beard
sits next to me
leaning his elbows
on the table
gumming a spoonful
of oatmeal.

i light a marlboro
fascinated by
the tattoo
that decorates
his forearm
with the image
of a dead angel
dangling between
the salivating jaws
of a golden retriever.

he pauses mid-chew
spoon still perched
to his lips
then startles me with
a sudden sideways glance.

he studies me for a moment
eyes wide, then says, "i
used to be the meanest
son-of-a-bitch south of hanoi."

he holds his gaze,
i nod in agreement
muttering "yep, i bet
you were uncle ernie. i
bet you were."

and i imagine he was
as i watch his grip tighten
around the spoon, causing
the limp angel to convulse
between the retriever's jaws.

Saturday Morning Cartoons

the living room
is blaring
with the clamor
of saturday morning
cartoons.

i'm hunched
on the couch
gorging myself
with fruit loops
while my brother
is in the corner
working over
grandma's poodle
with his latest
ninja turtle
techniques.

"i can't believe
john denver is dead,"
grandma sobs
as she performs
her slow-motion rendition
of the mime-christ,
head cocked sideways
palms extended

to the sky
in mock crucifixion.

grandpa sinks deeper
into his armchair
& knocks back
another shot
of vodka
as he strains
to stay focused
on the tv.

Interviewing Mr. Weck

the bedroom
is sibilant
with the whistle
& hiss
of congested
lungs.

an unshaded bulb
dangles from
the ceiling
& the shadows embrace
mr. weck's back
as he sits
on the edge
of the bed,
clutching his knees
to his chest.

he greets me
with a nod,
gestures for me
to sit down.

discarded sock puppets
litter the floor
& the air is tinged

with the scent
of sweaty palms

i place
my notepad
in my lap,
flip on
the recorder
& flash him
his cue.

"puppets are
my life," he says,
eyeing my argyles
as he dry washes
his knobby wrists
with slow,
fragile
movements.

At the Nursing Home

rumor has it
mrs. lapaglia
from room 102
has been ostracized
from the recreation hall
for calling false bingos,
& dickie kaplan,
that deaf-mute fella
from room 302
who spends every day
splayed on the floor
imitating gestures
of inanimate objects,
used to be a mime,
& old louise
from room 252
is accusing
the orderlies
of trying
to impregnate her
with sperm tainted enemas,
& mr. padgit,
the retired
drill instructor
from room 182
thinks his neck brace

is a clerical collar,
so he wanders
the halls
like a faith healer,
slapping the forehead
of every resident
he encounters.

Rush Hour in Chula Vista

the traffic is jammed
bumper to bumper
& the blazing sun glints
in all the windshields,
tossing dynamite
in my eyes.

the smell of exhaust fumes
intermingles
with the humidity,
causing my temples to throb
like a cunt-strangled cock
& the steering wheel is so hot
i've got a sunburn on my palms.

my wife fans herself
with the morning paper
while she fumbles
with the radio dial.

up ahead i notice
a pudgy mexican boy
wearing a pink wrestling leotard
with a matching shade of lipstick.
he gazes in my direction,
smiles, then blows me a kiss

as he arches his body
& performs a series
of clumsy pirouettes
toward my car.

an expression of terror
washes over my wife's face.
"oh my god, roll up the window,
lock the door," she said fishing
a can of pepper spray from her purse.

before i can react,
the pudgy mexican boy
is leaning in the window,
draping my ear
with burrito tainted breath.

"que pasa senor,
i'll let you wrestle me
for five dollar," he whispers,
running one slow finger
over my forearm.
i push his arm away
& tell him "no thanks."

the boy frowns, slams me
in a headlock, & plants
a kiss on my forehead.

"give me five dollar
or i'll tell the police
you like to touch little boys."

my wife screams & unleashes
with the pepper spray,
stunning the boy long enough
for me to wrench free
& roll up the window.

"but i love you harold," the boy
howls as he kisses the window,
streaking it with lipstick & drool.

my wife chokes back a tear,
& clears her throat. "how does
that boy know your name?"

i stare at the line of traffic
ahead of us, dab the sweat
from my face, & shrug.

Buttercup in a Pick-up Truck

the traffic on highway 101
is jammed bumper to bumper.
exhaust fumes & the humidity
envelope me
like a pair of
famished boa constrictors.
i snag the emergency flask of vodka
from the glove compartment
& take a couple swigs
to calm my nerves
when the stupid fuck behind me
driving the
rust & primer mottled pick up truck
with the tinted windows
decides to tap my bumper.
& just like that
my irritation swiftly blooms
into a full blown
road rage.
i fling open the door
step out
yank off my tie
& hurl it onto the hood
of the pick-up truck.
a moment later
the pick-up's engine belches

then issues an exhaustive hiss
& the driver climbs out.
he's a tall, gangly man
decked out in a pair of
hot pants & a halter-top
with the word 'buttercup'
stenciled across the front
& his hair
fashioned in
a neo-60s beehive
towers above his head
like a two-foot monolith.
he does a hasty
appraisal of it
in the side mirror
patting & tweaking
all the loose strands
back into place
but even after his best effort
a number of stubborn clumps
still jut from his head.
he slaps the mirror
cuts loose with a string of
"god damn mother fuckers"
then reaches into the bed of his truck
& pulls out a can of hairspray.
he shakes it
aims it at his head

presses the nozzle
but the can is empty.
frustrated
he chucks the empty can
into a nearby ditch
does an about face
& catches me staring.
"is there a fucking problem?" he asks.
"no," i say

slinking sheepishly
back into my chevy.
"there's no problem at all."

Sheltering Sheila

5:57 a.m.
the motel room
is still thick
with shadows.

i linger in bed,
pinned down
by the gravity
of a throbbing
hangover.

the distant sounds
of the highway
filter in
on the breeze
as sheila gazes
out the window
huddled over
a cigarette.

"baby killer!"
a voice shrieks
from the next room.
a door slams
& an argument erupts.

sheila flicks
her cigarette
out the window
& cups her palms
around her ears.

"sometimes, when
it's really quiet,
my hands sound
like the ocean,"
she says, focusing
her eyes
on the horizon.

Peristalsis in the Bowels of Downtown

all up & down
5th street there are
peep shows
coffee shops
liquor stores
& fresh tattoos that glow
on the pale
february bleached flesh
of girls
& all the skinny caramel lattes
are clutched too tight
even though they are hotter than
the august pavement
& everywhere you go
the cell phones are screaming
to be released from
all of the pockets, purses,
& glove compartment coffins
while a roving pack of mimes
stalk the corner of 4th & main
peddling
thespian nightmares
in a symphony of silence
so loud
it sounds like propaganda
& all the yellow

slowly leaks
from the sun
as i sit in the café
across the street
murdering myself
one cigarette
at a time.

The Butcher On Third Avenue (2001)

the butcher on third & vine
is a self-proclaimed
neo-nazi skinhead
who slaughters his cattle
with an old rusty blade
then collects their ears
in a mason jar
that is stashed
beneath his bed.
he stands 6'3"
thick neck
broad shoulders
& has 22 tattoos,
each depicting
dead farm animals
in various degrees of decay.

old mr. cohen,
stoop shouldered & skinny,
shuffles into the shop,
painstakingly propelled
by his hickory cane.
he greets the butcher
with a friendly tip of his hat.

"i am bovine van gogh,"

the butcher brags, smearing blood
stained hands across his apron. "what
can i get for you today, mr. cohen?"

mr. cohen cracks a nervous
grin & gestures at the hard salami.
"i'll take a pound of that," he says.

the butcher wraps & weighs
the meat, pushes it gently
across the counter,
then wedges a toothpick
between his teeth.
"that will be a buck
& a quarter," he says gazing lustfully
at the old man's enormous set of ears.

Maroon Chevy

6:37 p.m.
the café reeks
of dead matches
& stale cigarettes;
my mouth tastes
like a salmonella sandwich
& all i got is a cold cup of coffee
& yesterday's paper.

a bible study group
congregates at the next table,
there are at least a dozen of them,
young, tattooed, & pierced
sipping on skinny caramel lattes
& cappuccinos, their heads nod
in unison to a chorus of "amens"
while their eyes blaze
with pent-up holy-fire
begging to be released.

they join hands & engage in
a round of prayer
that gradually disintegrates into
conspiratorial whispers
stifled giggles

suspicious glances
& i am seized
by a sudden paranoia
& my imagination runs amok:
"are they a doomsday cult?"
"are they planting the seed of
a terrorist crusade for god?"

there is a tension in the air
as one of them points
at a maroon chevy
in the parking lot
& mutters something
about the offensive "darwin"
bumper sticker & how the owner
is going to burn in hell
& then there is a round
of hideous snickers, amens
& hallelujahs.

i get nervous & want to leave
but i am too afraid
because that is my maroon chevy
& i don't want to become a casualty
of their holy war.

Titanium Hip Concerto in C Major

late christmas eve,
a warped mozart album
warbles on the record player
as the party guests begin to leave.
i notice grandpa slumped
under the mistletoe,
shitfaced & disheveled,
eyeing everyone
with cynical amusement.
he knocks back another shot
of vodka & egg-nog
calmly shucks off
his sweat wilted t-shirt,
then snatches grandma
by the hair.
"hey everybody, listen to this,"
he says, pounding his knuckles
into grandma's newly constructed
titanium hip, "my brenda sounds like
a kettle drum!"
someone bumps the record player
& mozart screeches to a halt.
an eerie stillness fills the room.
all eyes are fixed on grandpa.
he continues pummeling
grandma's artificial hip;

the voracity of his punches
intensify with every blow.
the guests begin nudging each other
& whispering. one of them says, "sounds
more like a hollow cantaloupe than a kettle drum."
"i disagree," someone else says, "i think she sounds
like a soggy head of cabbage."
a thin sheen of sweat glistens
on grandpa's chest, shoulders, & arms
as he thumps at an ever maddening pace.
everyone continues to watch & listen.
a steady anticipation seems to build in the air.
"i think i can name that tune in 5 bruises or less,"
mrs. weaver shouts from the back of the room
& there is a gentle round of applause
as grandma slowly slumps to the floor.

The Danger of Deaf Bartenders

mitch rocks back and forth
on the barstool
nervous fingers fumbling with a cigarette
he eyes the woman next to him
admiring the long brown hair
that drools lazily from her scalp
over her shoulders
& spills across the back
of her tight blue dress.

he does a shot of whiskey
& works up the nerve
to talk to her.

buy you a drink, he says,
then is startled when he notices
she is wearing a gauzy surgical mask
the same shade as her dress.

she looks at him with bloodshot eyes,
blinks once, & tells him she will have
a rum & coke.

a panic steals over him
& he can't think
of anything to say

& he wonders how
she will drink the rum & coke
wearing that mask.

i am a dog breeder, she tells him,
i have successfully created
a chihuahua-pit bull hybrid
that i call the chi-bull.
they have proven to be
extremely popular
with the indigenous population
of northern mexico. i have a client there
who uses them for his lucrative
dog fighting business. he claims
that my chi-bulls are the fiercest, bravest
creatures he has ever had the privilege of owning.
at this point mitch is spooked;
he wants the conversation to end
so he orders the woman a rum & coke
but the bartender is half-deaf
& the batteries in his hearing-aid
haven't been changed since 1974.

Nicotine Wiggle of the Carcinogen Cowboy

what have
we become?

watch close
you might see
static positions
flowing through
a carpal tunnel syndrome

a voice lost somewhere
beneath the pillow
under the bed
behind the computer monitor

hidden sinkholes
in a virtual sandbox

a lustful breath drifts
from one strange mouth
to the next

violent erections scramble
the internet porn
while the carcinogen cowboy
does the nicotine wiggle

life is reduced to
a fistful of
palm sweat
& kung fu drizzle

the aroma of budweiser
& marlboro menthols
intermingle
as a voluptuous
cigarette butt bouquet
slowly blooms
in the ashtray
next to the computer.

Insomniac's Mantra

i want
to strangle
the sun
so the rest
of the world
can experience
the darkness
that dwells
inside
me.

Vicious Wishes

there's something
oddly attractive
about zoe.
perhaps it's
the way she
carefully
arranges the
angular
geometric features
of her face
on her head
every detail slightly askew
& a bit asymmetrical,
like a real life
living
breathing
flesh-toned
rendition of a
picasso painting,
always making
vicious wishes
with that
vicious gaze
while engaging you in
her cryptic
ouija-board
conversations.

Healthy Enough for Sex

every time
i talk to my
doctor about viagra
and if my heart
is healthy enough
for sex
he plugs a
lubricated finger
up my butt
and jiggles my
prostate.

Yesterday

yesterday
i reached
into my
breast pocket
and extracted
a magic
nipple wand
plunked it
between my lips
and nursed myself
back to
the present.

First Kiss Awkwardness

clumsily groping
each other
in the darkness
of a tin shed
her warm breath
delivers to me
the fruit-flavored
land of
lip-gloss wonder
as our mouths
press tight
& her tongue
greets mine
with all the
enthusiasm
of a splintered
popsicle
stick.

Darwinian Nuns & The Embryo Orphanage

atheists
disguised
as scientists
are breeding
darwinian nuns
in the embryo orphanage
while every night
somewhere
in the world
a remarkable 2.7 million
kamikaze moths
perish
as a result
of dive bombing
porch lights
& contrary to popular belief
9 out of 10
laboratory monkeys
prefer to copulate
missionary style
& an astonishing 35%
of all proctologists
moonlight
as puppeteers
& an even more astonishing
73% of puppeteers
moonlight
as proctologists.

Dangerous Night

i knew
it was going to be
a dangerous night
the moment i
caught a glimpse
of the swastika
tattoo
that swirled
around her
right nipple
like the blades
of a little
green
fan.

Art Lesson 101

gina set up
a canvas
below a tree
in her backyard
last spring
& let the birds
shit on it
for a week,
shellacked it
framed it
& sold it
at an art show
in soho
for $375.00.

Refrigerated Whispers Perpetuate the Revolution

250 million tongues
are shackled
to a cold
whisper

& all reasonable
correspondence
freezes
while

a deafening
silence
drenches the
carpet

& 3 lbs of headache
sinks into
a vat of
boiling
pancake batter.

the army
will eat good
tonight

even though

the mimes
refuse to
negotiate.

Expiration Date

we are all
as nourishing
yet soft
and vulnerable
as a loaf
of bread
with an expiration date
stamped on it...
check the mirror
and you might
find it.

Dangling at her Mercy

the gal
has a way
of making me
feel like a
golden earring
nestled within
the comfort of
her flesh
while dangling
millimeters
away from
certain
doom.

If I was an Ice Cream Flavor I'd be:

black & blue bruises
on the foot of a
podiatrist

midget clavicles
collected in a
hefty bag

the karate kid
enveloped in a
salmonella sandwich

herpes fumes
emanating from
a pubic bone
sonata.

Missing the Magic of My Youth

i can feel
yesterday's
gravity
dragging me back
deeper & deeper
with each
passing moment
as i struggle
to stay
focused
on tomorrow.

That Special Girl

she came
equipped with
a sexy set
of telepathic
eyebrows
that could
project
a mood
or thought
with the
slightest
twitch.

A Winter Poem

i often
scatter
leftover
kentucky fried chicken
in the backyard
on cold
winter days
just to watch
the birds
behave like
cannibals
(end poem)

We Are Art

we often
fail to realize
that merely existing
on this
floating rock
called earth
is an artform
and we all
should celebrate
our canvas
before the paint
runs out.

Burning Desire to Evolve

many of us
dive straight into
the fire of life
swim through
the flames
and wear
our burns
our scars
with pride
as we reach
the surface.

Over the Years

i have been the
clumsy comfort
sounding board
stepping stone
and one knight stand
in shining armor
for too many gals
as i lick my
own wounds.

Hangover 2017

i wake up
to discover croutons
in my buttocks
and quickly realize
the new year has already
made a tossed salad
out of me
as the sun
pisses its
golden gloom
all over me.

Every Damn Night

my dreams
spill out of my ears
soaking the pillows
with subconscious tornados
littered with
synaptic splinters
and broken relationships
that slowly fade
and dry up
as the sun
rises.

My Favorite Barfly

the multiple voices
that spill from
her skull
fit her
like thriftstore
lingerie
as she struts
her damaged goods
at the local watering hole
begging for drinks
and peddling her
tired story
like a treadmill
of sexy
misery.

Filling the Void

i do not
have a soul
i just
tap dance
shadow box
& jazz finger
my way
through the
daily chaos
called
life.

Crooked Smile 101

my liver aches
worse than
your broken heart
& i will always be
one shot of vodka
away from
you.

Ohio Boy Walkabout

i need
to walk
the path
barefoot
& absorb
the broken glass
that shimmers
like gems
among the
dirt & pebbles.

Fast Food Friend

i am nothing
more than
the wilting
lettuce
tomato
& rancid mayo
on your
big mac
whopper
& subway sammich
but you will
never forget
my flavor
& texture
as i
slide down
your
throat.

Affirmation of Self

i wander the streets
a hot headed gringo
stealing yawns
with jack off gestures
as my scalp itches
like a book of matches
begging for the friction
to make me
ignite.

Knock It Out of the Ballpark

we are all
walking the
last mile
minute by minute
hour by hour
day by day
year by year
like a
kung fu master
wearing
house shoes
saturated with
chloroform.

Lincoln's Beard

i gaze
at my reflection
in the tumbler
& sense
a mistake
blooming like
a bouquet
of raw spaghetti
in a pot of boiling water
as i fade into
the heat
of my 6th
diet coke & vodka.

Napalm Cochlea Enema

the muse pisses
in my left ear
& it trickles out
my nostrils
mouth
& down my throat
drowning me
one word at
a time.

The Letter "P" Pisses Me Off

why is the "p"
silent in pneumonia?
did an entity
urinate down your throat
while you slumbered?

why does the letter "p"
replicate the letter "f"
in pharmacy
phantom
photograph?

i say phuck-off
to my least favorite
letter of the
al"p"habet.

Barstool Philosopher

holding on to
a regret or two
is healthy
so long as
you learn from it
& don't allow
those demons to
possess you.

Nocturnal Cough Syrup Crusade

friday night
a quarter past twelve
found myself
huddled on the couch
knees drawn to chest
a mouthful of
diazepam, phenobarbital,
& several other anticonvulsants
with a bottle of
prescription strength
cough syrup
while i watched
the sleeves of uncle john's
snake-skin leather jacket
slither across
the living room floor
as it methodically gathered
bits of lint
& scraps of paper
for the nest
it was building
behind the refrigerator.

Throat Punch Butchers

taxes
traffic lights
politicians
doctors
lovers
auto mechanics
are all orchestrated
as a division of control
to drain
the brain fluid
out of your nose
like a chronic sinus infection
that leaves you
feeling
empty.

Oozing Crayola Red

got my face
laced up
like a raggedy andy doll
& frankenstein hybrid
then launched to the moon
in a rocket fueled by
fermented potato water.

Aggressive Swimmers

we are all at
a tipping point
yet we don't realize it
until we fall over the edge
& get lost in the plot
of life quicker than
the whip crack
of a flagellum.

She Was Known As Flipper

the gal was
all tits & torso
with stubby arms & legs
& was equipped
with a husky voice
that rattled my soul
as she drank me
under the table
& engaged in conversations
that would last until
the birds started singing
the good morning
song.

Tracing the Scars

i can feel
death massage
my scalp
as i grope
the dimensions
of the paper bag
reality has dealt
me today.

Bloodletting in the Hood

feign indifference
& embrace the moment
as confidence
& adrenaline surge
through every fiber
of your body
as you listen
to the trickle
of your life source
splatter on the sink
& floor.

The Twitch in My Tail

feeling feral
like a stray cat
that shits & pisses
where it wants
so don't force me into
a box of artificial dirt
simply to bury
my past.

The Social Badlands

opposites never attract
they simply conjugate verbs
on occasion
& then split an infinitive
in a petri dish
because every day
is a new
experiment.

A Flood of Circumstance

if you stare
hard enough
the avalanche of trash
blooms into
a beautiful
bouquet.

Picking at Scabs

she has a classic figure
that begs the eye to follow
yet you can't ignore
her suitcase hands
as she is always
lost in the fabric
of her brain folds
& you feel the bite
of her sudden
goodbye.

Fornication Flashbacks

there was a time
when we were
young hypersexual hedonists
swimming in
booze
bud
swing clubs
& libidinal madness
with nipple flesh mosaics
flickering in the
bluish light
of the tv
as the porno
illuminates each
lustful thrust
to the audience.

That One Date

her hands
smelled like
rancid bowling balls
that evening
& judging from the
strength of the scent
i would guess she
dipped her fingers into
a couple of
12-15 pounders.

Celluloid Serpent

we all
should earn
an oscar nomination
for channeling
our inner-cinema
& projecting it
upon the
world.

Better Than French Cinema

the gal
with the purple lipstick
half-shaven head
& blazing blue eyes
kept whispering
cryptic messages
in my ear
about einstein
bridging wormholes
behind mars
& that my maturity
will bleed to the surface
as she left my forehead & cheeks
riddled with a dozen
lipstick bruises.

Absorbing Her Aura

a woman decked out in
cowgirl is seated
at the table across from me
at the local coffeehouse

she thumbs through
an oversized picture book
featuring penguins

her lips move in whispers
while she reads the captions
then pauses ever so often
as she giggles & sips at her latte
& i find myself falling in love.

One of Those Nights

one of those nights
the heat & humidity
strips you of everything
clothes first
& then the memory
begins to trickle away
while visions of trucker mud flaps
the ones with the naked girl silhouette
mesmerized me with
its interstate undulations
waving back and forth
titties flapping
provocative
greetings
& goodbyes.

Braving the Storm

the community cum bucket
has no designs on me
so i develop a slight
fuckability complex
yet she is standing
a bit too close for comfort
so i take a step back
& radiate in the endless
series of radio silence.

Time to Dump the Garbage

it freaks me out that
disappeared & vanished
mean the same thing
so that is why
i speak sign language
with a german accent
as i cultivate my
mutton chops
because the
manual linguistics
gets complicated.

Perfectly Planned Catastrophe

gonna cash-in
the tax deductible
meteorite insurance
to patch the crater
the bleached blonde chick
from the local watering hole
carved into
my chest.

Social Sisyphus Syndrome

every other night
the gal treats me like
a temporary tattoo
as she talks with the
marlboro mouthed accent of
a dozen cheap beers
accompanied by a fleet
of whiskey & tequila
then discards of me
with a wad of toilet paper
& spit.

Be My Special Predator

ply with me
alcohol & mary jane
then grope me
like an epileptic
hellen keller
in a well lit room
& kiss me
fondle me
until my nipples bleed
into the mason jars
full of kentucky moonshine
that can be sold
via the underground
market.

Bitchy Cat

the tail broadcasts
her mood like a violent
umbilical cord
born from the
homicidal rage of a
karaoke rock star
who can't recite
the lyrics in synch
with the music.

The Cleansing

some shithead
with a perm
wearing a cyprus hill cap
keeps mean mugging me
from across the bar
like he's looking for an excuse
for me to take him to the
pugilistic prom in the
parking lot arena
so we can bleed
the booze out of our bodies
& reduce the
morning hangover.

Vices

everything is bleeding
one vice at a time
like the boiling oil from
a robot tranny hooker
that burns to the touch
& singes the soul.

21st Century Gladiators

the moral climate
is a digital wasteland
where we find ourselves
at the mercy of the keystroke
while we seek escape
via social media
like tunnel rats
scuttling through
the internet maze.

Inebriated Sacrifice

the universe expands
gravity fails me
& the concrete
bathes me in blood
as the colorful brutality
reminds me
i am the
drunken jesus.

Bloody Mop Wringer

please extract
& deliver
my liver
via priority mail
to a well stocked bar
after i pass into
the 4th dimension

he is my hero.

Forensic Plumber

nothing like
being startled awake
by a chick
who mumble-screams
"i am gonna drown in your
toilet bowl"
as she
barfs up
the crap booze
she inhaled
earlier at the local
watering hole.

Huff & Puff

vape me through
your special
mechanical device
& exhale violently
to exorcise your demons
the mold of your lips
never fit well
with mine
anyway.

My Vulcan Mojo

want my blood type?
want my social security number?
want my sperm count?
want my isbn number?
want my social status?
want my cell phone number?
want my cholesterol levels?
want my peanut butter & jelly recipe?
i have been rendered
an emotional
hemophiliac.

The Aftermath Equation

i have spent
far too many nights
hijacked by chicks
who pretend to be on the mend
as they slobber the shit
they think i want to hear
into my ear
fueling the moment
for another round of drinks
easing me into her ploy
before i realize
she is two shells short
of a rabid turtle.

Betty Crocker Shank

the cellophane thunder
of an american cheese slice
shatters
the fixtures of
my soul
as i absorb
the tongue wagging
of a sarcasm sandwich.

Damaged Goods Dominatrix

we plop onto the mattress
& she snuggles her head
onto my chest
& it appears her teeth
are sweaty
which is never a good sign

"we are perfection," she says

"think so," i reply.

"know so."

i take a deep breath
& tell her:
"i aspire to plant
a garden of snack cakes
that will eclipse both
the hostess & little debbie
empires combined."

she rapidly descends
into a snore
comprised of
the department of health
& mental hygiene
with a hint of vodka.

Chronic Sinusitis: I am a nasal cripple

my nose
embezzles
teeth
from my mouth
& sneezes out
the finest dishware
west of china

my nose explores
unholstered breasts
& lingers on
the erect nipples
of baby bottles

my nose
inhales germs
& weaves them
into colds

every time
i attempt
to sleep
my nose
loses nostrils
quicker than
i can breath

& no matter
where i go
i'm always
one step
behind
my nose.

Coffee at the Two-Cup-Café

my waitress
irene
is a
bull-dyke brunette
with a mouthful of cancelled teeth
& a smile
naked as
a sunday
sunbeam.

she leans
over the table
to refill the coffee
& i catch
an eyeful
of breasts
so close
i can feel the heat gathering
in her cleavage.

my libido makes
a hasty
alcohol addled
assessment:
"note...irene's breasts
pendulous but firm

not bad for a woman
pushing 50."

just then
the drunken sailor
at the next table
pinches her ass
she yelps
misfires
& i find myself
with a lap full
of scalding hot
columbian
breakfast blend.

she attempts to apologize
as i frantically fan
my crotch
but her voice
gets lost
somewhere else
as her face
is swallowed by
the phlegm basted
cackle
of a smoker's laugh.

Deaf Tone Bouquet

a dizzying strangeness
overcame me
when i lost my hands
while flirting with
an extremely attractive
deaf woman
at the local
watering hole
& spiraled into
an ear piercing
busy tone.

Phantom Girlfriend

she projected
the spotlight
upon me enough
to transform
me into
a shadow puppet
that would fade
when the clouds
rolled in
eclipsing the sun
& erasing me from
the sidewalk
or any other
faux stage
wall
or life performance
(End Act 2)

The Power of Words

got banned
from the local
watering hole
& escorted out
by a posse
of mean mugging
fellas & a loudmouth
chick hurling obscenities
so i flipped them
the peace sign
as i walked away

the scenario
felt shitty
but then i received
a call from a
gal pal
who said
i was adorable
which is an
endearing term
i have not heard
in over a
decade
& i melted
into a happy
place.

That Girl Holding A Can of Spam

see that girl
over there
in the
canned
food aisle?

i know
her

she is like
a vintage vcr

push the right
buttons
& you can
program her
to do
anything.

Confessions

gotta admit a bouquet of dandelions
is prettier than a dozen roses
gotta admit ted talks way gooder than oprah winfrey
gotta admit vehicles with plowing capacity are sexy
gotta admit knocking down dominoes
is funner than setting them up
gotta admit reese's peanut butter is better than jiffy
gotta admit soylent green is people
gotta admit abraham lincoln
is a better vampire slayer than buffy
gotta admit we are overdue for a world wide orgy.

Cluttered with Confusion

that gal
at the end
of the bar
wears her eyes
like a pair of bullet holes
that advertise
the condition
of her soul.

Special Night

she traces
my veins
& her touch
buzzes like
a jazz note
trapped in my
hip pocket.

Beware

i wanna
crumple you up
like a paper flower
then refold you
into a shape
that fits my
mold.

That One Gal

i want
to drag race
through the
drive-thru
of her soul
& order
the priciest
items on the
menu.

Sculpting an Identity

ruth is a
museum of memes
welded together
from all of the clever thoughts
of other folks
as she constructs
her wall of fame.

Dive Bar Therapy

willie is a
barfly prophet
always predicting
the fate of his
next drink with
impeccable accuracy
as he winks out into
the edge of the bar.

A Bar Full of Poetry

scanning the faces
at the local watering hole
i see folks
anxious to spill
their stories
with each passing
drink.

The Ventriloquist

today is
just another
spooky
puppet show
set to a
disembodied
voice.

Apartment Life Curse

it's getting
hard to distinguish
the loud voices
emanating from
across the hall
& the voices rattling
in my head.

On the Brink of a Crisis

i realize
life has become
creepier than
an episode of
the twilight zone
while finger
banging my
emotions into "submission"
as i read a "mad magazine."

The Beds We Make

hiding the pain
is worse than
eating shoe leather
while sleeping on the
couch & fantasizing
about the threadbare
spandex of a
helicopter mom.

That Life Thingie

slices swifter
than an eyeball
papercut
hits harder
than a mike tyson
uppercut
pronounces you dead
before 6 feet
of dirt
smothers the
flesh jacket.

Running to the Grave

the roll of quarters
in my pocket
waits patiently to
shatter a jaw
bust open
& scatter across
the ground
like a waterfall
of classic washington
arcade game credits.

Art of the Sucker Punch

the scabs eventually
crust off
revealing the contours
of a fresh scar
that adds another
paragraph to the narrative
of your life.

Brass Knuckles

i have more
in one hand
than your face
can handle
so step away
& allow me
to enjoy
my drink.

Embezzling Kisses in the Rectory

father o'sullivans bible
is leaking miracles
as he huddles
over a playboy
in the bathroom
of the rectory
embezzling kisses
from the fellatio
sculpted lips
of the centerfold
clutching the mattress
face down
ass up
sleek body taut
as her shoulder blades
pierce her back
like a pair
of ivory steeples.

A Different Lens

every bottle
is a journey
that holds its
secret wisdom
as it glides down
the gullet & hugs
you from the inside
out.

I Never Suffer

i embrace
the chaos
& bask in it
like a post-coital
cuddle.

Slow Burn

her pigtails
tickle my thighs
& whisper secrets
on my belly
as i become
lipstick war paint
beneath her gaze
& the music guides us
through another night.

Hand Grenades of Infatuation

intellectual
blind spots
echoing into
the past
like shattering glass
as the gal molds me
into a by-product
of cancel culture.

Mapping the Anatomy of Lust

her smile
fades into
a slow tongue swallow
as the air charges
with radio static
& boot camp amnesia
while the street lamps
slowly fade into
gallows.

Diving Into Divorce

i was treading
the depths of daily life
as the tide
slowly swept me
out into the horizon
where nothing
looked or felt
familiar anymore.

Time Clock Cancer

the numbers
on my calendar
keep rearranging themselves
creating new days
new months
new years
as they slowly reveal
an alternate reality.

Mirrors

your eyes
meet your own
blazing implosions
of ego captured
in a cracked mirror
as the narrative
rises to the surface
& spills onto the
linoleum.

Chucking the Fallen Fruit

she craved
conversations filled with
lowfat guilt
to help shed
those nasty pounds
of depression.

The Art of Suffering

there's nothing
quite like
the sight
of a blank canvas
planted on an easel
begging for the stroke
of the brush
to bring it
to life.

Ambient Charm

life is a
razorblade parade
full of booze
brawling & broads
& some days
it will make
you cry.

Swallow Your Feelings

rolling pennies
a poor man's set
of brass knuckles
while getting
mired down by
the same old shit
all around the
jar of vaseline
a graveyard to a pair of
stray pubes
a dead fly
& a slippery soul.

Perpetual Trick or Treat

my life resembles
a neverending rack
of halloween lights
shining bright
with every cut,
bruise & excuse
to have another
drink.

Tug Job

the gal keeps me
in the orbit of
her boobies & smile
while we yawn
at the blistering rate
of moral decay
& the booze saturates
the carpet like a lazy
waterfall of disappointment.

Lethal Night

i smell death
on her breath
a combo of whiskey
beer & cigarettes
that cascades my face
like a baptism
of debauchery.

Finding Comfort

i feel so alone
sometimes it is
like a lovestruck
companion.

Fixed Bayonet

she has
x-ray eyes
behind those sunglasses
constantly
reading me
& calculating her
next move to capture
my attention & guide me
in her direction.

Razor Blade Theology

force feed me
the knuckle sandwich
so i can attain
the proper sustenance
i didn't attain
from my halloween candy.

Truth Be Told

i excel at
making bad decisions
as the mid-life crisis
slithers past me
since i am not even
palatable to the
serpents.

Two Spliff Whif

catch my drift
in a butterfly net
& place it beneath
your pillow
every night.

Real Gone Chick

the gal was
tragically hip
as if being cool
was some debilitating
disease she dealt
with on a day-to-day
basis while her pigtails
slithered from her scalp
like a pair of copperhead
snakes.

Untitled

there is something special
about the first time
your eyes meet
that makes your heart flutter
& shocks your body with
electric adrenaline
as it lays the mapwork
for the evening...

Absorbing the Glow

the gal
is perched
on the veranda steps
studying the glow
of the flashlight
through her fingertips
as she hums
the same tune
as the mosquitoes
that autograph her flesh
with venomous
tattoos.

Recognize Your Shadow

she lurks
in the shadows
of the crosshatch
a murky
comic book-esque
femme fatale
waiting to lure me
into her inky
web.

The Pulse of Poetry

i see the words
as living, breathing
pulsing & veiny creatures
begging to be plunked
onto the page
& made tangible
to the rest
of the universe.

Running with the Jackals

they call me
the cackle jackal
as i take a pull
from the bottle
of cheap vodka
that scours my throat
like steel wool
& reminds me
i'm alive.

Take a Peek

i plant
bad days
in the compost heap
out back & watch
them bloom into
tiny beacons
of hope.

Silent Echo

shelly's eyes
brim with tears
as she points a finger
at the words stuck
in her throat
like a pistol
& her writhing tongue
articulates nothing
except mute agony
that sails along her breath
& crashes into
the january air.

Lip Gloss Lust

my lips
are stitched
by the flavor
of you.

Ragged Morning

the inside
of my eyelids
look like death
& my nostrils
reek of gluten free
porcupine smiles.

Kung Fu Cowboy

set the rules
on fire
& ink your own
manifesto
using poetry
as a shameless
currency.

Duck Season

ducking bill collectors
ducking ex-lovers
ducking telemarketers
ducking punches
ducking bad relationships
ducking the police
ducking intellectual snobs
ducking promises
ducking commitment
ducking cans of spam
ducking my way
straight into
a lincoln's beard.

Deriving Sustenance

hit that bottle
harder than
a linebacker plowing
over a ballerina
as you subsist
on bread sandwiches
with a splash of vodka
& wake up feeling
taken out like the trash
as you celebrate prom
in the suffocating confines
of a garbage can.

Things Remembered

found the words
i lost
during the great
tongue probe
of 1991
lips locked
in a lust fest
while exchanging words
in a breathless
symphony of moans.

Fortune Cookie Logic

confucius says:
your deodorant
has magnetized
a secret
nostril.

Spent Matches

i don't know how
to tell time anymore
i simply stare
at clocks via candlelight
& shrug as the night
unravels
to witness
what bounty
the sun
will bring.

Terminal Floatation

they called the fella
two pack tonto
on account he smoked
at least two packs
of unfiltered cigarettes
per day as he coughed
up a lung
strapped it to his back
& floated into his home town
of albuquerque
like a cilia propelled
dirigible.

Smothered By It

a swelling
of self awareness
feels like
static positions
in a confetti blizzard
stitching hidden
sinkholes into
a sandbox
paranoia slinks & slithers
a dark nameless thing
pulsing in the corner.

100 Dead Babies

the conductor's wand rises
suspended in the air
a speechless moment
as 100 dead babies
wail away in mute harmony
on the floor of the
orchestra pit & the audience
sways gently to the rhythm
of the thunderous air conditioning
unit.

The Ones You Notice

the gal had
a thrift store physique
with her angular
geometric features
everything slightly askew
a living, breathing picasso
painting that radiated
beauty.

Absorbing the Locals

spent the day
people gazing
at the local walmart
snatching the fading
embers from their
tribal fire.

Mending the Discord

the gal
has a voice
like a pair of dice
tattling in a tin cup
but her laugh & smile
provides the salve
for the soul
that blots out
the daily chaos
& unleashes
a cosmic sexiness.

Two Seats Over

she is a princess
of emptiness
blowing kisses
that miss by a mile
& making promises
that are as empty as
a vampire's coffin
at midnight.

Brain Twitch

bitten by
a sleeping pill
& a shot of vodka
i listen to myself
breathe while calculating
the trajectory
of a sock puppet
incubating beneath
the bed.

Riding the Buzz

creativity erupts
in rapid thought spasms
an ejaculation
of the imagination
while clouds collide
with mountains
outside the window.

The Way She Flows

the gal plucked
the rubber bands
from her pigtails
& her hair spilled
across her shoulders
like a whisky waterfall
gushing over
the dam.

No Way to Escape

when i am
in her orbit
the gravitational pull
of cheap booze
traps me in
a sink or swim
situation
where drowning
is the only
solution.

Jukebox Blaring & Booze

the brunette gal
with the punk rock stylings
the booze on her breath & a pall mall
perched between her lips
leans in seductively
whispers into my ear,
"you have toilet paper
stuck on your shoe."
she smiles & winks
as she glides off
to the other side
of the bar
& giggles with
her posse of girlfriends.

Soccer Moms are Toxic

the starbucks is abuzz with
the vicious sibilance
of latte swilling
soccer moms
as they engage in
a round of gossip
i glance around
at all these
faces full of pancake rumble rouge
& maybeline maybes
the toxic ambiance
is almost overwhelming
can't stand the crowd here
all of these women are so cold & cloudy
with a 78% chance of rain
i palm the $5 tip she leaves
on the table
& use it to buy
a vodka & diet at the bar
across the street.

Making Subtle Power Moves

trapped in the life
of a hardcore
sapiosexual
i crave your dreams
the taste of your mind
the drench of your ideas
as you smother me
in your vocabulary.

A Symphony of Ridicule

i am slouched on a bench
at the local mall
gnawing on a corndog
when a young
impish girl
does a series of
clumsy pirouettes
then stops in front of me
stares for a moment
points & laughs
& i could already detect
at least a dozen
cruel remarks
stitched into
the curves of her
kool-aid mustache.

Under Her Breath

have spent
the past three hours
watching
the gal sitting in
the corner booth
where a
naked bulb
dangles above
her head
carving shadows
on her face
her dark
sunken eyes
stagger in
their sockets
as dim faces
flicker past
the café window
a dying moth
flutters
in tiny circles
next to the
smoldering ashtray
as she whispers
descriptions
of her favorite

magazine ads
under her breath
& forges them
into haikus.

Ozone Layer Innuendo

"throw away
your aerosol sprays,"
the experts said
back in the
summer of 1976,
"cause the cfcs are eatin'
a hole in the ozone layer."
but i'm here
to tell ya'

that ain't no hole
in the ozone layer
up there...
that's the
gaping vagina
of mother earth
come to fuck
us all.

Living on the Fringe

i am nothing
but a victim
of my own
decisions
& can live
with that because
i am having fun
along the way.

At the Bus Stop

my ears burn
with the serpentine
hissss...of radial tires
that hug the
soggy memories
of her cotton candy
colored hair
waving goodbye
in the breeze.

Innocence Lost

if only
love was
still as simple
as you writing
our names
encapsulated
in a heart
pierced by an arrow
on the cover of your
trapper keeper.

The Light Fades

don't seek
warmth here
my fire
has grown small
mere embers
that sparkle & pop
as it launches
red glowing dots
into the night sky.

Where the Fleas Sleep

we tend
to die
of something
boring
every damn
day.

Toxic Relationship

at times
a relationship
is forged
under the bite
of your fingernails
in the palm meat
of your fist
as you struggle
to find the calm place.

Chalk Lines Fade

the blue eyed gal
at the edge of the bar
finally fell silent
as she chewed
on my soul
like beef jerky
& spit it into a napkin
then left for the bar
across the street.

Starbucks Tourette's

i once spent
an entire day
inserting the words
"ligature asshole"
into conversations
with strangers
between sips of
my vodka spiked
grande mocha.

Dead Page

stabbing
a writing journal
with a dead pen
proves to be cathartic
when the ink
refuses to flow.

Here Comes the Flood

emotional intelligence
is the toughest
brain-stuff
to master
because the heart
always interferes.

Icky Rules

time is ours
to mold
into whatever
shape
we desire.

Wrinkles & Scars

dancing with my demons
day by day
minute by minute
as i fall deeper
into the funk
where everything
is a little broken
& i have to climb
through the brambles of
doubt to escape.

This is the Damn Poem

This is the poem procured from the excrement
of Oprah Winfrey's book of the month
This is the poem found coursing through the
irritable bowels of a Shetland pony
This is the poem hijacked from sweat drenched
bar stools and strangled rectal meat
This is the poem gleaned from the pituitary gland
of a morbidly obese beautician

This is the poem brimming with
intimacy issues and palm sweat
This is the poem full of tube sock ejaculate
This is the poem that tickles your throat
like a slow tongue swallow
This is the poem forged from projectile vomit
and feminine itch products
This is the poem supplemented with
big-breasted sluts in gangbang action
This is the poem that bleeds on the carpet
every time you read it upside down
This is the poem wilting in the rusted-out trunk
of a '76 Chevy Nova
This is the poem that tastes like
a "no money back" guarantee

This is the DAMN poem
no one will publish.

in his own words:

Brian Fugett is a member of the slacker, fast food generation that has been branded with an 'X' by that Canadian-born, literary terrorist known as Douglas Coupland. Meanwhile, he sits in his pad all day consuming more oxygen than he's worth. He's been doing it for over 35 years now and has become quite efficient at it. Eating and voiding are the only things he really knows how to do. Between meals and trips to the shitter, he covertly milks 'West Nile Virus' from the tits of pregnant mosquitoes and uses it to butter the toast of local politicians. He is the editor/publisher of *Zygote in My Coffee*.

"The brilliance of these poems will break your heart, due to a voice silenced too soon. Yet, the humanity breathing off the page will bring a smile to the face of even the most hardened hearts. If this is to be Brian Fugett's swan song, it's a most beautiful melody."—Michael N. Thompson, author of *A Murder Of Crows* and *Verbal Alchemy*

୭

"Brian's voice in these poems alternates between hilarity and nihilism. The hilarity is natural and infectious and the nihilism is matter of fact. The tone reminds me of a book I return to again and again whenever I am feeling my most disconnected from and most disenchanted with my fellow humans. *Psychotic Reactions and Carburetor Dung* by the brilliant Lester Bangs. I only met Brian in person once, at a karaoke bar in Ohio in 2011. But I loved him and I'm grateful that he is still here in these kick life in the balls poems."—Misti Rainwater-Lites, author of *Clown Gravy* and others

www.ingramcontent.com/pod-product-compliance
Lightning Source LLC
Chambersburg PA
CBHW022128080426
42734CB00006B/272